Easy Phonics

The Woodpecker's Project

and other stories

V Short OO

3c

by Tapasi De

Illustrated by Suman S. Roy

ABOUT PHONICS

Phonics is the understanding that there is an important relationship between the letters or graphemes of the written language and the individual sounds or phonemes of the spoken language.

A strong knowledge of phonics helps a child considerably to recognize these relationships, to recognize familiar words accurately and automatically, and also "decode" new words. This knowledge substantially improves the reading ability of the child.

In the *Easy Phonics* series, the basic 48 sounds of English have been dealt with through stories. The series is divided into 4 levels with 4 books in each level. Each book contains 2-3 stories based on a particular sound. Colourful illustrations and the repetition of a particular sound ringing through the story make this series absolutely unique!

CONTENTS

A STUDY TOUR WITH MISS VANESSA

V as in VAN

The sun rose in the valley. Violet and Veronica were sharing the same room in the hotel.

They had come to Venice on a study tour. Ms. Vanessa, their geography teacher, had come with them too.

Violet looked out of the window. A veil of mist covered the morning sky. Violet and Veronica had two more friends in their group. They were Victor and Vince.

The boys were very enthusiastic. At nine o'clock a voice was heard, "Children, get ready fast!" It was Ms. Vanessa. 'We will first go to a vineyard.

And off they went in a van. They craved to see the wine plants, though they knew that Ms. Vanessa would not allow them to taste.

The grape-bearing vines appeared to be happily smiling at the sun! Veronica and Violet walked amidst the vines.

A little later, the children got back into the van. Vicky and Victor were busy learning the names of the various wines that were made there.

Ms. Vanessa told the driver that their next place of visit was Cave Verge.

They drove down quite a long distance until they reached Cave Verge. There was a massive waterfall near the cave.

"Oh, what a big waterfall! And that's Cave Verge, isn't it? Come on, let's go inside," said Victor.

The children bravely moved into the huge cave. The cave had lovely, carved natural rock formations inside it.

The rocks inside had patches of brown, red, green and mauve. The children and their teacher were surprised to see these strange motives.

It was late afternoon. Ms. Vanessa gave lunch packets to the children. The packets had vegetable chops, vanilla pudding and sandwiches.

Finally, the day was over. It had been an eventful day. Ms. Vanessa heaved a sigh of relief that the tour had gone well.

Words with the 'V' sound

give	dove	have	shove
valve	active	olive	resolve
vehicle	achieve	leave	prove
above	love	nerve	solve
serve	groove	Venus	viper
violin	volcano	vote	vulture
vest	village	vinegar	verb

THE WOODPECKER'S PROJECT

OO as in LOOK

Woopie the woodpecker was busy making a project. She was sitting in her room searching for facts. She tried looking it up on the internet, but it did not help.

So Woopie called her mom and said, "Mom, what should I do? How do I complete the project?" Her mom, who was cooking, brought her a bowl of cookies.

Woopie's room was a bit untidy at that time. Storybooks and guidebooks were scattered around her. A fish hook hung on the wall.

“Woopie, why don’t you go to the city library and look for books there? But take a bath and have some food before you leave,” said her mom.

And so, a little later Woopie put on a woolly frock. She said goodbye to her mom and flew away to the city library.

The library was near a brook. Woopie had never been to a library before. She looked all around and saw books everywhere!

There were tall bookcases full of books of various colours and sizes. Woopie noticed that many students were reading; no one talked!

Woopie went to the good-looking otter sitting at the counter. He was the librarian. He gave her a membership card and requested her not to talk.

Woopie walked slowly, scared that the sound of her footsteps may disturb other people. She tiptoed to the bookshelves and looked for the books she wanted.

She looked through many types of books like encyclopedias, picture books, journals and travel books. While reading, she also noted down points in her notebook.

Woopie spent an hour at the library. When she was leaving, the librarian gifted her a beautiful bookmark.

Woopie flew over the brook. She looked down and saw many of her friends walking on the footbridge. Finally, she reached home and completed her project.

Words with the short 'OO' sound

poor	flood	good	cook
wood	book	woof	foot
rook	shook	stood	took
crook	bookkeeper	look	checkbook
hood	goodnight	football	overlook
woodland	scrapbook	footprint	mistook
unhook	textbook	wooden	outlook
footage	rookery	footpath	

LET'S RECALL

1. Who was Ms. Vanessa?
2. What did the children see in the vineyard?
3. Which place did they visit after the vineyard?
4. What did the lunch packets given by Ms. Vanessa contain?
5. Where did Woopie's mother suggest her to go so that she could complete her project?
6. What did Woopie wear to go to the city library?
7. What all did Woopie notice in the library?
8. Who was the librarian and what did he give to Woopie?